BRITISH RAILWAYS STEAMING ON THE WESTERN REGION

Volume Three

Compiled by
PETER HANDS & COLIN RICHARDS

DEFIANT PUBLICATIONS
190 Yoxall Road
Shirley, Solihull
West Midlands

Printed in the United Kingdom by Netherwood Dalton & Co. Ltd., Huddersfield, England.

CURRENT STEAM PHOTOGRAPH ALBUMS AVAILABLE
FROM DEFIANT PUBLICATIONS

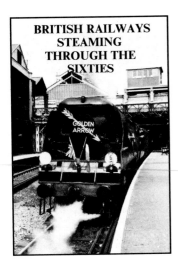

VOLUME 3
A4 size - Hardback. 100 pages
-182 b/w photographs.
£7.95 + 75p postage.
ISBN 0 946857 02 4.

VOLUME 4
A4 size - Hardback. 100 pages
-182 b/w photographs.
£7.95 + 75p postage.
ISBN 0 946857 04 0.

VOLUME 5
A4 size - Hardback. 100 pages
-180 b/w photographs.
£7.95 + 75p postage.
ISBN 0 946857 06 7.

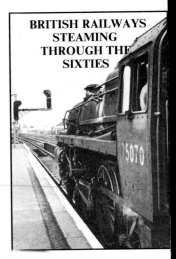

VOLUME 6
A4 size - Hardback. 100 pages
-182 b/w photographs.
£8.45 + 75p postage.
ISBN 0 946857 08 3.

VOLUME 7
A4 size - Hardback. 100 pages
-182 b/w photographs.
£8.45 + 75p postage.
ISBN 0 946857 10 5.

VOLUME 8
A4 size - Hardback. 100 pages
-181 b/w photographs.
£8.95 + 75p postage.
ISBN 0 946857 14 8.

VOLUME 9
A4 size - Hardback. 100 pages.
-182 b/w photographs.
£9.95 + 75p postage.
ISBN 0 946857 18 0.

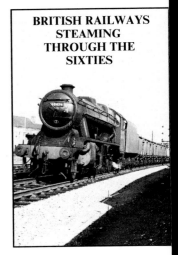

VOLUME 10
A4 size - Hardback. 100 pages.
-182 b/w photographs.
£9.95 + 75p postage.
ISBN 0 946857 20 2.

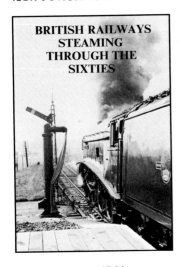

VOLUME 11
A4 size - Hardback. 100 pages
-180 b/w photographs.
£10.95 + 75p postage.
ISBN 0 946857 24 5.

BRITISH RAILWAYS STEAMING THROUGH THE SIXTIES

IN PREPARATION

VOLUME 12

BRITISH RAILWAYS STEAMING ON THE EX-LNER LINES

VOLUME 1
A4 size - Hardback. 100 pages.
-187 b/w photographs.
£9.95 + 75p postage.
ISBN 0 946857 19 9.

BRITISH RAILWAYS STEAMING ON THE EX-LNER LINES

IN PREPARATION

VOLUME 2

CURRENT STEAM PHOTOGRAPH ALBUMS AVAILABLE
FROM DEFIANT PUBLICATIONS

VOLUME 1
A4 size - Hardback. 100 pages
-180 b/w photographs.
£8.95 + 75p postage.
ISBN 0 946857 12 1.

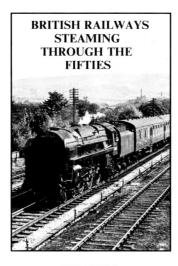

VOLUME 2
A4 size - Hardback. 100 pages
-180 b/w photographs.
£8.95 + 75p postage.
ISBN 0 946857 13 X.

VOLUME 3
A4 size - Hardback. 100 pages
-180 b/w photographs.
£9.95 + 75p postage.
ISBN 0 946857 16 4.

VOLUME 4
A4 size - Hardback. 100 pages
-180 b/w photographs.
£9.95 + 75p postage.
ISBN 0 946857 17 2.

VOLUME 5
A4 size - Hardback. 100 pages
-180 b/w photographs.
£9.95 + 75p postage.
ISBN 0 946857 22 9.

VOLUME 6
A4 size - Hardback. 100 pages
-180 b/w photographs.
£9.95 + 75p postage.
ISBN 0 946857 23 7.

BRITISH RAILWAYS
STEAMING
THROUGH THE
FIFTIES

IN
PREPARATION

VOLUME 7

BRITISH RAILWAYS
STEAMING
THROUGH THE
FIFTIES

IN
PREPARATION

VOLUME 8

VOLUME 1
A4 size - Hardback. 100 pages
-188 b/w photographs.
£7.95 + 75p postage.
ISBN 0 946857 03 2.

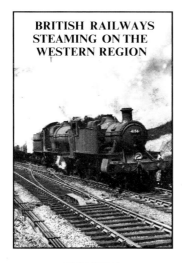

VOLUME 2
A4 size - Hardback. 100 pages
-181 b/w photographs.
£8.45 + 75p postage.
ISBN 0 946857 11 3.

VOLUME 3
A4 size - Hardback. 100 pages
-179 b/w photographs.
£10.95 + 75p postage.
ISBN 0 946857 25 3.

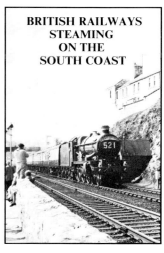

IN
PREPARATION
MARCH 1990

CURRENT STEAM PHOTOGRAPH ALBUMS AVAILABLE
FROM DEFIANT PUBLICATIONS

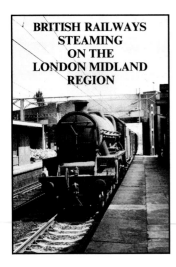

BRITISH RAILWAYS STEAMING ON THE LONDON MIDLAND REGION

VOLUME 1
A4 size - Hardback. 100 pages
-184 b/w photographs.
£7.95 + 75p postage.
ISBN 0 946857 05 9.

BRITISH RAILWAYS STEAMING ON THE LONDON MIDLAND REGION

VOLUME 2
A4 size - Hardback, 100 pages
-181 b/w photographs.
£8.95 + 75p postage.
ISBN 0 946857 15 6.

BRITISH RAILWAYS STEAMING ON THE LONDON MIDLAND REGION

VOLUME 3
IN
PREPARATION
MARCH 1990

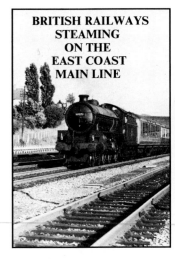

BRITISH RAILWAYS STEAMING ON THE EAST COAST MAIN LINE

A4 size - Hardback. 100 pages.
-183 b/w photographs.
£8.95 + 75p postage.
ISBN 0 946857 07 5.
(Reprinted July 1988)

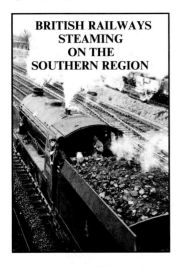

BRITISH RAILWAYS STEAMING ON THE SOUTHERN REGION

VOLUME 1
A4 size - Hardback. 100 pages
-188 b/w photographs.
£8.45 + 75p postage.
ISBN 0 946857 09 1.

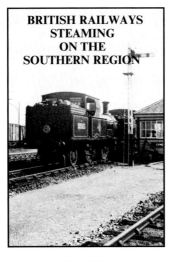

BRITISH RAILWAYS STEAMING ON THE SOUTHERN REGION

VOLUME 2
A4 size - Hardback. 100 pages
-181 b/w photographs.
£9.95 + 75p postage.
ISBN 0 946857 21 0.

BRITISH RAILWAYS STEAMING ON THE SOUTHERN REGION

IN
PREPARATION

VOLUME 3

BRITISH RAILWAYS STEAMING THROUGH PETERBOROUGH

A4 size - Hardback. 100 pages
-163 b/w photographs.
£10.95 + 75p postage.
ISBN 0 946857 26 1.

OTHER TITLES AVAILABLE FROM DEFIANT PUBLICATIONS
PRICES VARY FROM £1 to £3.80 INCLUDING POSTAGE

WHAT HAPPENED TO STEAM
Volume One
THE GREAT WESTERN
2800 Class 2-8-0's
&
R.O.D. Class 2-8-0's

WHAT HAPPENED TO STEAM

This series of booklets, 50 in all, is designed to inform the reader of the allocations, re-allocations and dates of withdrawal of steam locomotives during their last years of service. From 1957 onwards and finally where the locomotives concerned were stored and subsequently scrapped.

BR STEAM SHED ALLOCATIONS

This series lists all individual steam locomotives based at the different parent depots of B.R. from January 1957 until each depot either closed to steam or closed completely. An attractive bookbinder is available for this thirteen book series.

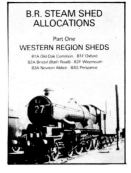

B.R. STEAM SHED ALLOCATIONS
Part One
WESTERN REGION SHEDS
81A Old Oak Common · 81F Oxford
82A Bristol (Bath Road) · 82F Weymouth
83A Newton Abbot · 83G Penzance

WHAT HAPPENED TO STEAM
Volume Twenty Eight
THE L.M.S.
8F 2-8-0's
&
Somerset and Dorset
7F 2-8-0's

WHAT HAPPENED TO STEAM
THE L.N.E.R.
B1 4-6-0's.

B. R. STEAM SHED ALLOCATIONS
Part Eight
SCOTTISH REGION SHEDS
60A Inverness · 60E Forres
61A Kittybrewster · 61C Keith
62A Thornton Junction · 62C Dunfermline
63A Perth · 63D Oban
64A St. Margarets (Edinburgh) · 64G Hawick
65A Eastfield (Glasgow) · 65J Fort William
66A Polmadie (Glasgow) · 66D Greenock (Ladyburn)
67A Corkerhill (Glasgow) · 67D Ardrossan
66A Carlisle (Kingmoor) · 68E Carlisle (Canal)
St. Rollox Works

B. R. STEAM SHED ALLOCATIONS
Part Seven
NORTH EASTERN REGION SHEDS
53A Hull (Dairycoates) · 53E Goole
54A Sunderland · 54D Consett
55A Leeds (Holbeck) · 55G Huddersfield
55A Wakefield · 56G Bradford (Hammerton St.)

ACKNOWLEDGEMENTS

Grateful thanks are extended to the following contributors of photographs not only for their use in this book but for their kind patience and long term loan of negatives/ photographs whilst this book was being compiled.

T. R. AMOS
TAMWORTH

H. H. BLEADS
BIRMINGHAM

B. W. L. BROOKSBANK
LONDON

N. L. BROWNE
ALDERSHOT

L. BROWNHILL
BRIERLEY HILL

R. S. CARPENTER
BIRMINGHAM

J. K. CARTER
MILLHOLME

D. COLES
HIGH WYCOMBE

KEN ELLIS
SWINDON

A. N. H. GLOVER
BIRMINGHAM

J. D. GOMERSALL
SHEFFIELD

RAY HARRIS
NEW MALDEN

PETER HAY
HOVE

J. HEAD
EASTBOURNE

R. HENNEFER
SUTTON COLDFIELD

M. F. HIGSON
THE SMOKEBOX

R. W. HINTON
GLOUCESTER

H. L. HOLLAND
ST. CATHERINES, ONTARIO, CANADA

F. HORNBY
NORTH CHEAM

A. C. INGRAM
WISBECH

L. C. JACKS
BIRMINGHAM

D. K. JONES
MOUNTAIN ASH

R. J. LEITCH
SAWSTON

BRIAN LESLIE
BEACONSFIELD

TERRY NICHOLLS
BRISTOL

D. OAKES
HITCHIN

R. PICTON
WOLVERHAMPTON

W. POTTER
BISHOPS CLEEVE

N. E. PREEDY
HUCCLECOTE

B. G. PRICE
WOLVERHAMPTON

P. A. ROWLINGS
ALCONBURY

K. L. SEAL
ANDOVERSFORD

G. W. SHARPE
BARNSLEY

JOHN SMITH
LENS OF SUTTON

A. SWAIN
WEMBLEY

D. TITHERIDGE
FAREHAM

T. WALKER
CHEPSTOW

KIT WINDLE
LOWER BREDBURY

Front Cover — Churchward 4700 Class 2-8-0 No 4705, from 82B St. Philips's Marsh, departs from the loop at Cowley Bridge Junction, Exeter, in a flurry of steam, with a rake of up coal empties on 14th April 1962. Behind and to the right of the semaphores is the river Exe. (Terry Nicholls)

ISBN 0 946857 25 3

© P. B. HANDS/C. RICHARDS 1989
FIRST PUBLISHED 1989

INTRODUCTION

BRITISH RAILWAYS STEAMING ON THE WESTERN REGION — Volume Three is the third such album to concentrate on the Western Region from the 'British Railways Steaming Through the Sixties' stable.

These books are designed to give the ordinary, everyday steam photographic enthusiast of the 1950's and 1960's a chance to participate in and give pleasure to others whilst recapturing the twilight days of steam. In this particular album there are some thirty-eight contributors.

Apart from the main series, individual albums will be produced from time to time. Wherever possible no famous names will be found, nor will photographs which have been published before be used. Nevertheless, the content and quality of the majority of photographs used will be second to none.

This third album contains a wide and varied selection of photographs of steam at work and rest from many different locations on the Western Region from 1948-1966 when allocated steam finished on this region. Unless otherwise mentioned, all locomotives in this album are of Great Western origin.

The majority of photographs used in this album have been contributed by readers of Peter Hands series of booklets entitled 'What Happened to Steam' & 'BR Steam Shed Allocations' and from readers of the earlier 'BR Steaming Through the Sixties' albums. In normal circumstances these may have been hidden from the public eye for ever.

The continuation of the 'BR Steaming' series etc., depends upon you the reader. If you feel you have suitable material of BR steam locomotives between 1948-1968 and wish to contribute them towards the series and other future publications please contact either:

Peter Hands,   Colin Richards
190 Yoxall Road,   28 Kendrick Close,
Shirley, Solihull,   OR   Damson Parkway, Solihull,
West Midlands B90 3RN   West Midlands B92 0QD

CONTENTS

STATIONS AND WARNING NOTICE

1) A fine view of the layout of the south end of Princes Risborough station on a sharp and clear winter's day in 1958. Although everything looks Great Western, at one time it was once jointly owned by the Great Central Railway. (Brian Leslie)

2) This warning notice, which speaks for itself, was originally issued in 1861 by the Taff Vale Railway Company. One would think, in later years, that the new masters (GWR and British Railways) would have seen fit to provide a new notice instead of blacking out TAFF VALE. Taken at Llandaff on 21st May 1955. (N. L. Browne)

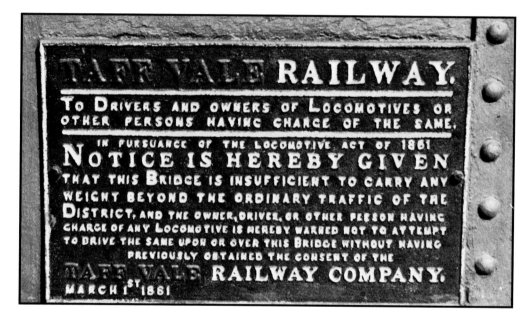

TAFF VALE RAILWAY.

TO DRIVERS AND OWNERS OF LOCOMOTIVES OR OTHER PERSONS HAVING CHARGE OF THE SAME.

IN PURSUANCE OF THE LOCOMOTIVE ACT OF 1861

NOTICE IS HEREBY GIVEN

THAT THIS BRIDGE IS INSUFFICIENT TO CARRY ANY WEIGHT BEYOND THE ORDINARY TRAFFIC OF THE DISTRICT, AND THE OWNER, DRIVER, OR OTHER PERSON HAVING CHARGE OF ANY LOCOMOTIVE IS HEREBY WARNED NOT TO ATTEMPT TO DRIVE THE SAME UPON OR OVER THIS BRIDGE WITHOUT HAVING PREVIOUSLY OBTAINED THE CONSENT OF THE

TAFF VALE RAILWAY COMPANY.

MARCH 1ST 1861

3) A splendid shot of Newton Abbot station, taken from the road bridge, looking towards the London direction in 1957. This was an extremely busy place in steam days and once had its own locoshed and workshops which are hidden to the extreme right of this picture. (H. H. Bleads)

4)   Awaiting its next duty, 4500 Class 2-6-2T No 4507 (72C Yeovil), sizzles, astride an inspection pit at Taunton on 12th May 1962. These small wheeled tank engines were ideal for branch line work and were to be seen over many of the secondary lines of the old G.W.R. system before the mass invasion of the d.m.u's. 4507 was in the twilight of its career and was withdrawn from Yeovil shed in October 1963, which by then was the property of the Western Region. (Terry Nicholls)

5) Cardiff (General) was a fabulous place to be in steam days, with a never ending stream of expresses, local passengers and freights. 4300 Class 2-6-0 No 6320, from 82D Westbury, climbs into the station with a lengthy express from the Newport direction on 15th September 1958. Waiting for the road on a centre track is 7200 Class 2-8-2T No 7226 (87D Swansea East Dock), in front of which is an unidentified *Castle* Class 4-6-0. (N. L. Browne)

6) *Modified Hall* Class 4-6-0 No 7918 *Rhose Wood Hall*, for many years a favourite inmate of 84E Tyseley, commences the ascent of Hatton Bank, between Warwick and Lapworth, with an eight coach down express – circa 1956. Three other examples of this particular series were based at Tyseley at this stage in time, these being Nos 7908 *Henshall Hall*, 7912 *Little Linford Hall* and 7913 *Little Wyrley Hall*. (N. E. Preedy)

7) The old Somerset & Dorset Railway, absorbed by the Southern Railway and later the Southern Region, was taken over by the Western Region authorities in February 1958. Steam was to dominate all lines associated with the S & D until final closure in March 1966. On 16th October 1965, BR Class 5 4-6-0 No 73001 (82F Bath Green Park) tackled the long climb up to Masbury summit, near Chilcompton, with the 9.00 am Bristol to Bournemouth train. (Ken Ellis)

8) After the summer service ceased in 1962 and following the mass withdrawals of many types of Western passenger engines in September of the same year, many of the survivors were relegated to more menial duties on the main lines radiating from Paddington. *Castle* Class 4-6-0 No 7021 *Haverfordwest Castle*, from 81A Old Oak Common, was captured by the camera at Sonning cutting with an up parcels train on 11th August 1963, one month away from withdrawal. (F. Hornby)

9) A lengthy row of gaunt terraced houses, high on a hill-side, look down upon the small two road shed at 87H Neyland, in June 1963. Outside the depot were two unidentified 5700 Class 0-6-0 Pannier Tanks and a 4300 Class 2-6-0. Neyland shed had opened in 1856 but was to close three months after this picture was taken. The surviving allocation of steam locos were transferred to Whitland, which in turn closed in December 1963. (N. L. Browne)

10) Collett 'Dukedog' 4-4-0 No 9011 (built at Swindon in 1937), once named *Earl of Ducie*, on shed at 81D Reading on 14th June 1953. On this date, 9011 was based at Swindon for use over the M & SWJR lines and remained in service until July 1957. These engines, with their outside frames and swirling rods, were extremely popular with enthusiasts and were often to be found on specials hired by the same. (N. L. Browne)

9

11)   Two 86E Severn Tunnel Junction based locomotives, in tandem, on 25th May 1963. 5101 Class 2-6-2T No 4130 pilots
        2800 Class 2-8-0 No 2862 as they labour up the incline from the Severn Tunnel, at Pilning, with a short but fully laden
        coal train. A large number of 2-6-2 Tanks from the 3150, 5101 and 6100 classes were allocated to Severn Tunnel Junction,
        in its heyday, mostly for use as pilots through the formidable tunnel. (Terry Nicholls)

12)   Steam fills the atmosphere on a gloomy and misty 10th April 1957 at 81C Southall. Standing outside the shed, ready for
        their next tasks, were 1400 Class 0-4-4T No 1436 and 6100 Class 2-6-2T No 6156. Both engines were allocated to Southall.
        Time was running out for 1436, being taken out of service in October 1958. 6156 was destined to survive until December
        1965 when it was withdrawn from 81F Oxford. (N. L. Browne)

13) Many of the Docks system of railways had their own engine sheds, even well into British Railways ownership and they employed masses of tank engines to shunt the vast yards. Nowadays, with the road-rail container traffic, the necessity for such depots is all but obsolete. Newport, in South Wales, had its own docks shed at Pill, coded 86B. Out of steam on 27th May 1956 was 5700 Class 0-6-0PT No 5714. (N. L. Browne)

14) Towards the end of Western steam, all pretence at keeping up any form of cleanliness was all but abandoned, as can be seen by this photograph of *Hall* Class 4-6-0 No 5992 *Horton Hall* (85B Gloucester - Horton Road) at Worcester with a local passenger train in April 1965. Devoid of name and shed plates, *Horton Hall*, was in disgraceful external condition. It was withdrawn from 86B Newport (Ebbw Junction) in August 1965. (D. K. Jones)

11

15) Although not as yet officially withdrawn, it is doubtful if any of the wheels on this trio of 'Dukedog' 4-4-0's, in store with sacked chimney's at 89A Oswestry on 26th May 1957, ever turned in revenue earning service again. From right to left are: Nos 9020, 9026 and 9010. Facing 9010 is an 89C Machynlleth 2251 Class 0-6-0 No 2255. The three 'Dukedogs' were all condemned between July and August 1957. (F. Hornby)

16) 84C Banbury based *Hall* Class 4-6-0 No 4942 *Maindy Hall* stands on a through road at Hereford on 25th May 1957 with the stock of a local passenger train. *Maindy Hall*, constructed at Swindon in July 1929 was paired with a Hawksworth tender when this photograph was taken. It was transferred away from Banbury in June 1960 and served at a further five sheds before being withdrawn in December 1963 and is now in safe hands at GWS Didcot. (F. Hornby)

17) The vastness of Birmingham (Snow Hill) is shown quite clearly in this picture which was taken on 20th July 1961. This (Wolverhampton) end of the station was all but deserted as 5700 Class 0-6-0PT No 3660, from 84E Tyseley, drifted through, light engine. At the far (London) end of the station, the platform was filled with passengers awaiting the arrival of a Wolverhampton to Paddington express, still in the hands of steam. (D. K. Jones)

18) 81A Old Oak Common once boasted a large allocation of 0-6-0 Pannier Tanks, mostly for the haulage of empty stock trains to and from Paddington but by May 1963 their numbers had been somewhat reduced. One of its fleet of 9400 Class locomotives No 9411 was photographed in the yard at Old Oak, out of steam. Note that 9411 was still sporting the old 'Lion & Wheel' logo. This engine survived until the end of steam at 81A June 1965. (Ray Harris)

19) A massive piece of coal is balanced precariously on the tender of BR Class 9F 2-10-0 No 92217, a visitor from Tyseley, as it drifted around the shed yard at 81D Reading on 21st September 1964. Constructed in 1959, 92217 was first based at 86C Cardiff (Canton) and during its brief career was also allocated to Banbury, Old Oak Common and St. Philip's Marsh as well as Tyseley, from whence it was condemned in August 1966. (D. K. Jones)

20) Two 'foreigners' pose alongside the shed building at 87J Goodwick (Fishguard) in June 1963, three months prior to closure to steam. Hiding amidst the shadows is *Hall* Class 4-6-0 No 5903 *Keele Hall* (87F Llanelly), in company with BR Class 5 4-6-0 No 73023, also from Llanelly. *Keele Hall* also demised in September 1963 but 73023 was to soldier on until April 1967 by which time it was at 9K Bolton, on the London Midland Region. (N. L. Browne)

21) A soot-stained lower quadrant heralds a free passage for Churchward 4300 Class 2-6-0 No 5317, from 84B Oxley (Wolverhampton), as it prepared to leave Acton yard, in the immediate vicinity of Paddington, with a fitted freight on 1st October 1955. These 2-6-0's with their light axle weight, were able to work over most lines on the Western Region system, mostly on local passengers and freights. (F. Hornby)

22) A grubby *Hall* Class 4-6-0 No 4983 *Albert Hall*, based at 86C Cardiff (Canton), reverses on to the main line at Bristol (Temple Meads) after being serviced at 82A Bristol (Bath Road) in June 1959. Withdrawn from 82B St. Philip's Marsh in December 1963, *Albert Hall* lay rotting at Barry Docks from June 1964 to October 1970 until it was 'rescued' by the Birmingham Railway Museum. Many years on and *Albert Hall* is still not fully restored. (N. E. Preedy)

23)   An idyllic scene in rural England on 16th June 1962. Fluffy white clouds in the distance threaten the bright sunshine as
Churchward 2800 Class 2-8-0 No 3838, with steam shut off, emerges from Sapperton tunnel with a lengthy freight, bound
for Gloucester and South Wales. 3838, a longstanding inmate of 86E Severn Tunnel Junction, was transferred to 81E
Didcot in June 1964. This was followed by a final move to 81C Southall four months later, with condemnation following
in November of the same year. (N. E. Preedy)

24)   5700 Class 0-6-0PT No 9638, allocation not known, simmers gently in the peace and quiet of the small yard at Brecon on 26th July 1949, after marshalling a cattle train – note the shunting pole wedged in the cab-side handrail. Still in G.W.R. livery, 9638 was one of the updated 8750 series, with an enlarged cab, boiler top feed, larger windows and cab-side shutters. Brecon goods yard, on the Central Wales line, closed in 1955. (A. N. H. Glover)

25)   A begrimed 4500 Class 2-6-2T No 4564, based at the near at hand 85B Gloucester (Horton Road), wheezes and creaks as it slowly hauled a lengthy rake of mineral wagons, bunker-first, through Gloucester (Eastgate) station on 9th March 1964. Allocated to Horton Road, from 83D Laira (Plymouth) in September 1963, 4564 was to survive until September 1964. Gloucester (Eastgate) closed in 1975 but the adjacent Central station is still open. (B. W. L. Brooksbank)

26) A massive amount of coal has been fashioned into a pyramid shape in the tender of a very clean 87F Llanelly based *Grange* Class 4-6-0 No 6844 *Penhydd Grange*, as it stood under the lengthy footbridge in the yard at 86C Cardiff (Canton) in 1957. *Penhydd Grange* was drafted to 87A Neath in November 1961 but it returned to Llanelly nine months later. Withdrawn from Llanelly in April 1964, 6844 was scrapped by Cohens, Kettering. (G. W. Sharpe)

27) The large complex at Shrewsbury shed was originally owned jointly by the GWR & LNWR. Under BR it was run by the LMR authorities from 1948-1949, thereafter it came under the control of the Western Region. Up until the mid-sixties, ex. GWR and LMR engines were a common sight until the demise of Western steam. Two LMR locos were noted in the yard on 29th March 1953 – Class 4F 0-6-0 No 44600 and Class 6P5F Stanier 2-6-0 No 42950. (A. N. H. Glover)

28) The former Great Western/Great Central station at Beaconsfield on the once proud main line from Paddington to Birmingham, hosted 2251 Class 0-6-0 No 2246, as it headed homewards on a centre road with an Acton to Banbury freight on 30th July 1957. 2246 departed to new ground in December 1957, being re-allocated to 81E Didcot, where it remained until drafted to 85A Worcester in October 1960. (Brian Leslie)

29) Double-heading of express passenger trains was a once common sight between Exeter and Plymouth in steam days, the fearsome banks at Dainton, Hemerdon and Rattery being the common denominator. *Manor* Class 4-6-0 No 7820 *Dinmore Manor* pilots *County* Class 4-6-0 No 1015 *County of Gloucester* near to Ivybridge with an excursion on 30th May 1959. Both locomotives were allocated to 83D Laira (Plymouth). (J. Head)

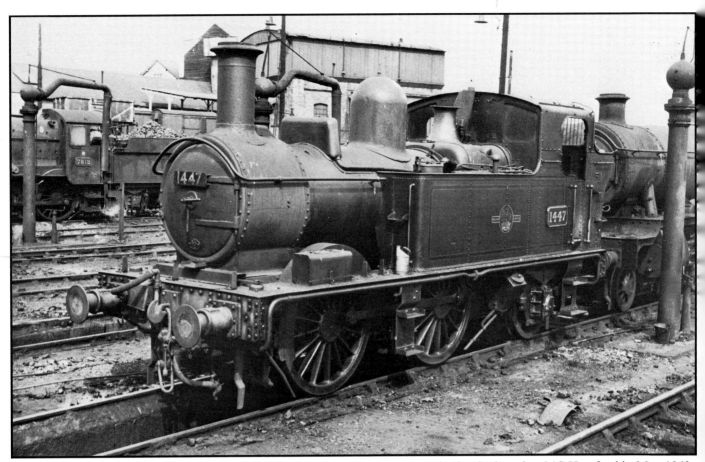

30) A locally based 1400 Class 0-4-4T No 1447 was captured by the camera in the shed yard at 86C Hereford in May 1963. The photographer had obtained the permission of the shedmaster for 1447 to be towed out of the shed to be photographed, a rather nice gesture. To the left of 1447, near to the coaling stage, was *Manor* Class 4-6-0 No 7812 *Erlestoke Manor*, now preserved on the Severn Valley Railway, but then based at 89A Shrewsbury. (Ray Harris)

31) BR *Britannia* Class 4-6-2's Nos 70050-54 were all allocated to 66A Polmadie (Glasgow) in Scotland, from new. By January 1963, all had found their way to 5A Crewe (North) on the London Midland Region. On 2nd May 1964, one of their number – No 70050 *Firth of Clyde*, still based at Crewe (North), found itself at work on the Western Region, at West Wycombe, being employed on an F.A. Cup Final special. (D. Coles)

32)   Once the pride and joy of the Great Western, the *King* Class 4-6-0's were to remain intact until No 6006 *King George I* was withdrawn in February 1962 and then it was a rapid downhill road to oblivion for the remaining members. Hard at work on 26th August 1961, was No 6022 *King Edward III*, from 84A Wolverhampton (Stafford Road), at West Bromwich, with an up Wolverhampton to Paddington express. 6022 was withdrawn in September 1962. (T. R. Amos)

33)   A cramped scene in the shed yard at 84G Shrewsbury in 1960. An unidentified *Modified Hall* Class 4-6-0 is partially hidden between *Manor* Class 4-6-0 No 7811 *Dunley Manor* and *Hall* Class 4-6-0 No 6944 *Fledborough Hall*, both of which were stabled at Shrewsbury. *Dunley Manor* moved away to 89B Croes Newydd in September 1961. *Fledborough Hall* had departed to 86C Cardiff (Canton) in September 1960. (G. W. Sharpe)

34) Newbury is more famous for its links with the racecourse and the once common 'Ban The Bomb' protesters, than for its railway connections. Nevertheless it is an important link in the overall rail network. Drifting into the station on a summer's day in 1959, was *King* Class 4-6-0 No 6018 *King Henry VI* (81A Old Oak Common) with a down express. BR Class 4 2-6-0 No 76064 (71A Eastleigh) waits to depart with a Didcot to Southampton local. (R. S. Carpenter)

35) Ex. Rhymney Railway P Class 0-6-2T No 82 seen awaiting cutting up in "C" Shop at Swindon Works on 13th June 1954. It had been withdrawn the previous month, from Cardiff East Dock. The "C" Shop and concentration yard at Swindon had opened in 1932, for dealing with scrap, including the cutting up of locomotives and was situated at the western end of the works yard. Equipment included a crane of 25 tons capacity and other plant. (A. N. H. Glover)

36) No longer needed by its former masters, *Hall* Class 4-6-0 No 4917 *Crosswood Hall*, stands nameless, numberless and coalless outside 82D Westbury on 14th July 1963, a rainy, drab day which makes the plight of 4917 even more dismal. Withdrawn from Westbury in September 1962, *Crosswood Hall* was to remain in store there until about May 1964, when it was sent for cutting up at Cashmores, Newport. (D. K. Jones)

37) A splendid and unusual view of Aberbeeg as taken from a lofty viewpoint above the station on 26th May 1956. The puffs of white smoke indicate that 6400 Class 0-6-0PT No 6415, from 86A Newport (Ebbw Junction), was departing with the 6.42 pm auto-train to Ebbw Vale. The Brynmawr lines lead off to the right of the picture, under the canopy. Aberbeeg station, of Great Western origin, closed to passenger traffic in 1962. (N. L. Browne)

38) One of the erstwhile Hawksworth heavy shunting 9400 Class 0-6-0 Pannier Tanks based at 81A Old Oak Common, No 9405 threads its way gingerly through the maze of lines and pointwork leading into the vast station at Paddington on 19th May 1962, with the stock of a down express. Transferred to 81D Reading in July 1964, 9405 returned to Old Oak Common the following month. A final transfer in March 1965 took it to 82E Bristol Barrow Road. (R. J. Leitch)

39) A filthy, soot encrusted *Hall* Class 4-6-0 No 6951 *Impney Hall*, heads homewards tender-first, with a short bulk cement train at Wolvercot (Oxford) on 23rd August 1963. 84C Banbury, by now under the tender mercies of the London Midland Region authorities, managed to cling on to *Impney Hall* until October 1965, when it was drafted to 2A Tyseley and condemned two months afterwards. (T. R. Amos)

40)   Although surviving in service until March 1965, most enthusiasts will remember the brief but famous periods of time that BR Class 9F 2-10-0 No 92220 *Evening Star* spent on the Somerset & Dorset Railway, based at 82F Bath Green Park in 1962 and 1963. Much of its time was spent hauling the celebrated *Pines Express* and it was noted, complete with the same headboard 'on shed' at Green Park on 8th September 1962. (N. E. Preedy)

41)   The end of the road for 4500 Class 2-6-2T No 5565, dumped unwanted on a side road at 89C Machynlleth on 10th September 1960, after being condemned the same month. Note the damage to the safety valve casing etc. Later this same month 5565 was despatched to Swindon, where it lay in store for approximately three months. A final journey took 5565 to South Wales and oblivion at the hands of Cashmores, Newport. (L. C. Jacks)

42)   A rainswept scene at Launceston on 21st October 1961. A member of the footplate crew closes a tank cover, after his charge, 4500 Class 2-6-2T No 5572 (83D Laira – Plymouth) had taken refreshment after arriving with a local passenger from Plymouth. 5572 was withdrawn from Laira in April 1962 and stored there until around November of the same year. It then rotted at Barry until August 1971, being saved for posterity by GWS Didcot. (Terry Nicholls)

43) 1400 Class 0-4-2T No 1435, built at Swindon in 1934 at a cost of £2,247, prepares to leave 83C Exeter (St. Davids) prior to working the Exe Valley auto-train service to Dulverton via Tiverton and Morebath Junctions on 20th August 1953. Six members of this class were shedded here for this specific purpose, with a further two being sub-shedded at Tiverton Junction. (A. N. H. Glover)

44) Most signals were situated on the 'correct' side of the lines which trains were approaching on, unless there was a 'blind' spot on a bend. The latter appears to be the case at Keynsham, between Bristol and Bath. *Hall* Class 4-6-0 No 6937 *Conyngham Hall*, from 81E Didcot, leaves the station, under clear signals, with the 7.00 pm express from Temple Meads, on 6th September 1964. (R. Picton)

45) This excellent photograph personifies the rural railways of Britain. 5101 Class 2-6-2T No 4157 (86G Pontypool Road) prepares to take on water supplies at Quakers Yard (High Level) station, whilst in charge of the 1.00 pm local passenger from Pontypool Road to Neath on 12th June 1964. The station buildings, overbridge, signalbox, water tank and small lower quadrant signal all help to complete the scene. (W. Potter)

46) An absolutely filthy *Hall* Class 4-6-0 No 6940 *Didlington Hall*, from 85B Gloucester (Horton Road), had just left the tunnel at Cattybrook with a lengthy Class 8 loose-fitted freight on 5th September 1963. Note the peculiar signal arrangement of the lower quadrant signal and its post, to the left of the train. Despite its begrimed external condition, *Didlington Hall* was to continue in service at Horton Road until condemned in May 1964. (R. Picton)

47) 2800 Class 2-8-0 No 3812, allocation not known, traverses freshly ballasted track as it skirted the sea wall with a down Class 8 loose-fitted freight train, near to Teignmouth on 4th June 1953. In comparison to most other parts of the Western Region network, freight traffic in this part of the region was comparatively light, especially during the busy summer months. (D. K. Jones)

48) A fine view of Beaconsfield station on 17th August 1958. 6100 Class 2-6-2T No 6165, based at 81C Southall, departs from the station with the 9.30 am Princes Risborough to Southend-on-Sea excursion, consisting of ten carriages of mixed stock. The fact that 6165 was travelling bunker-first points to the possibility that the rostered locomotive had failed or there was a dire shortage of motive power. (Brian Leslie)

49)   A row of water columns appear to be on guard duty in the shed yard at 81C Southall on 15th May 1963. Lined up in front of the running shed are six locomotives, three of which can be identified as 9400 Class 0-6-0PT No 8456, *Modified Hall* Class 4-6-0 No 6967 *Willesley Hall* and 6100 Class 2-6-2T No 6133, all allocated to Southall. The other three engines belong to the 6100, *Hall* and *Manor* classes. (Peter Hay)

50)   A totally deserted platform at Coryton Halt (South Glamorgan) on 21st May 1955. A smartly turned out 6400 Class 0-6-0PT No 6416, from the former Taff Railway shed at Cardiff (Cathays), coded 88A, was ready to push its train, auto No 3, back to Cardiff (Bute Road). 6416 spent its last few years of service based at 88D Merthyr, being withdrawn from there in September 1963. It was cut up at Swindon Works two months later. (N. L. Browne)

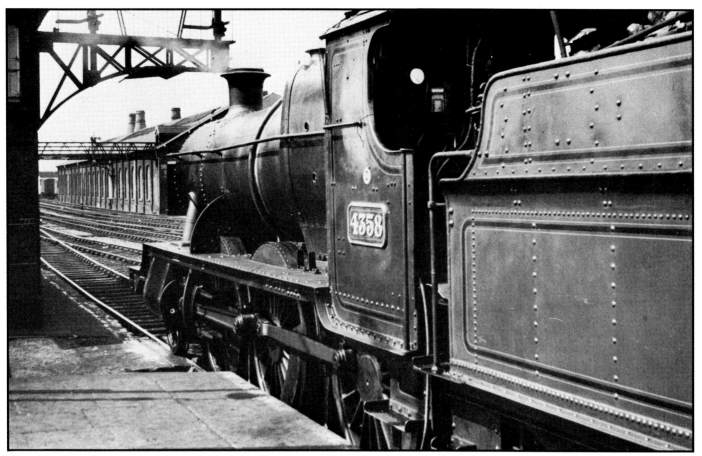

51) Looking in superb external condition, Churchward 4300 Class 2-6-0 No 4358, from 85B Gloucester (Horton Road), was photographed from an unusual angle at Hereford whilst in charge of a northbound passenger train on 25th May 1957. 4358 was one of just three surviving members of the 4300 series, the others being Nos 4375 (84F Stourbridge) and 4377 (89C Machynlleth). (N. L. Browne)

52) 8100 Class 2-6-2T No 8109 and WD Class 8F 2-8-0 No 90483, in steam outside their local shed at 84D Leamington on Saturday 26th July 1958, awaiting their next duties. This small, four road shed had been opened by the GWR in 1906. It was taken over by the LMR authorities from the Western Region in 1963 and recoded 2L in September of the same year. The shed closed on 14th June 1965. (J. D. Gomersall)

53) Posing for the camera, two members of the shed staff at 83D Laira (Plymouth) are dwarfed beneath the frames of a Laira based *Castle* Class 4-6-0 No 4089 *Donnington Castle*, photographed alongside the shed building in June 1949. The lettering of its new owners are stencilled on the tender and *Donnington Castle* had been fitted with a front numberplate (home-made). (G. W. Sharpe)

54) *Modified Hall* Class 4-6-0 No 6997 *Bryn-Ivor Hall*, allocated to 82B St. Philip's Marsh, leans to a curve as it coasted through Ashley Hill, Bristol, descending Filton bank, with the 4.36 pm Cardiff to Portsmouth Harbour express on 3rd May 1963. Judging by the dwindling supplies of coal in the tender of *Bryn-Ivor Hall*, it would be replaced by another locomotive upon arrival at Temple Meads. (Terry Nicholls)

55) Another *Modified Hall* Class 4-6-0, this time in the shape of No 7910 *Hown Hall*, from 81C Southall, passes the yards at Acton with an up china clay fitted freight train from Cornwall on 6th May 1961. *Hown Hall* remained at Southall until November 1963, moving on to 81A Old Oak Common. A further move took 7910 to 81D Reading in May 1964, with a final transfer to 81F Oxford five months later. It was withdrawn in February 1965. (F. Hornby)

56) The 1101 Class 0-4-0 Tanks were built by the Avonside Engineering Company for the Great Western Railway in 1926 and were designed specifically for dock shunting. No 1104 was photographed outside the brick built shed at 87C Danygraig on 7th June 1953. All six members of this class were based at Danygraig and they were withdrawn from service between November 1959 and January 1960. Also in this picture is 5700 Class 0-6-0PT No 8720. (F. Hornby)

57) A fine spring day at Grange Court Junction on 25th May 1957. *Hall* Class 4-6-0 No 5988 *Bostock Hall*, based at 87E Landore (Swansea), had paused briefly with the 10.30 am local stopping train from Swansea to Gloucester (Central). *Bostock Hall* moved to the Midlands in March 1960, to 84C Banbury. Apart from a spell at 81A Old Oak Common between October 1962 and June 1963, 5988 was to remain in the Midlands until withdrawal. (F. Hornby)

58) There was not much time for the signalman at Tigley to take a break during steam days, with a constant stream of trains battling their way up Rattery bank in the summer months. *Hall* Class 4-6-0 No 6938 *Corndean Hall* (83A Newton Abbot) assists *King* Class 4-6-0 No 6027 *King Richard I* (83D Laira - Plymouth) over the gradient with the down *Cornish Riviera* express, from Paddington to Penzance on 29th June 1958. (J. Head)

59) A 'Scottie' dog peers from one of the station billboards as 1600 Class 0-6-0PT No 1623, from 85B Gloucester (Horton Road) runs round its train at Cinderford on 25th May 1957, prior to returning to Gloucester. Cinderford, once the property of the Severn and Wye Joint Railway, closed during 1958. 1623 fared much better, surviving in service until June 1965, being withdrawn from 87F Llanelly. (N. L. Browne)

60) 84E Tyseley based 4300 Class 2-6-0 No 5369 was a long way from its Birmingham home when photographed at Aberystwyth station on 15th July 1958. 5369 was being employed on the 9.55 am local passenger to Shrewsbury. It was re-allocated to 82B St. Philip's Marsh in October 1960, moved on to 82C Swindon in September 1961, back to 'The Marsh' in August 1962 and to its last home at 86G Pontypool Road, a month later. (F. Hornby)

61)   Shrouded in steam, Churchward 4700 Class 2-8-0 No 4702, allocated to 81C Southall, restarts a lengthy down freight from a signal check on one of the slow lines at Acocks Green, in the outer suburbs of Birmingham in March 1962. 4702 was almost at the end of its working life, being condemned in June 1962. After a period of storage at Southall and Swindon, 4702 was scrapped at Swindon Works in November 1962. Note the tall, wooden posted signals which were a common feature along this stretch of the main line to Paddington. (P. A. Rowlings)

62)   A view of the station at Southall, as taken from the long footbridge which leads to the nearby locoshed on 2nd November
1963. Watched by a handful of spotters from one of the platforms, *Grange* Class 4-6-0 No 6841 *Marlas Grange*, a locally
based engine with painted smokebox hinges, negotiates pointwork. Behind *Marlas Grange* is 2800 Class 2-8-0 No 3820,
a visitor from 81E Didcot. (J. K. Carter)

63)   Churchward 4300 Class 2-6-0 No 6307, home shed not known, in the yard near to the coaling plant at 84A
Wolverhampton (Stafford Road) on 12th March 1949, fifteen months after nationalisation. 6307, built at Swindon in
1921 and fitted with outside steampipes, ended its days at 84J Croes Neydd, being condemned in July 1960. It was
scrapped at Wolverhampton Works the same month. (A. N. H. Glover)

64) With two of the locomotives featuring in the last two photographs being associated with the shed at Croes Newydd, we pay a visit to the same on 30th August 1959. Most of the engines in this picture are from the 2251 Class 0-6-0's and 4300 Class 2-6-0's. Nearest the camera is 5378, a local engine. Immediately to the left of 5378 is 2275, from 89C Machynlleth. 5378 was withdrawn the following month. (F. Hornby)

65) Towards the end of 1965 steam was in its death throes on the Western Region. On 13th November the shed yard at 81F Oxford was packed, with rows of lifeless leviathans, not a wisp of live steam in sight. Amongst the ex. GWR engines, there was a stranger in the camp, an unusual visitor from 41J Langwith Junction – WD Class 8F 2-8-0 No 90258. Although not officially condemned until January 1966, the end had arrived for 90258. (D. Titheridge)

66)   With the driver sitting comfortably, BR Class 3 2-6-2T No 82041 (82F Bath Green Park), approaches the camera with a local stopping train at Mangotsfield on the outskirts of Bristol in February 1964. In January 1957 ten of these engines were based at 88C Barry, these being Nos 82003/35-37/40-44. All were transferred to English sheds by August 1958. 82041 went to 82A Bristol (Bath Road) in June 1958. (G. W. Sharpe)

67)   The former Great Western lines in Devon and Cornwall were amongst the first on the Western Region to be cleared of steam with most express passenger workings in the hands of diesel power by the end of 1962. A few short years earlier, on 24th June 1958, 1400 Class 0-4-2T No 1434 was being employed on an auto-train at Plymouth (North Road). 1434, a local engine from 83D Laira, survived in service there until July 1962. (N. E. Preedy)

68) Many sheds from all regions continued with the old bucket and hoist system of supplying locomotives with coal, right up until closure of the depots concerned. A filled bucket hovers above LMS Class 3 2-6-2T No 41231, prior to the contents being discharged into the bunker of the same at 84H Wellington on 12th April 1960. 41231, a local inhabitant of Wellington moved on to new ground at 84D Leamington in October 1961. (B. W. L. Brooksbank)

69) We move to the far flung reaches of the Western Region, to Milford Haven in West Wales where a less than clean *Hall* Class 4-6-0 No 4927 *Farnborough Hall* (87F Llanelly) was eking out its last weeks of revenue earning service. On 5th June 1963 it had steam to spare whilst engaged, tender-first, on shunting duties. Built at Swindon in May 1929, *Farnborough Hall* was condemned in September 1963. (F. Hornby)

70) Within a matter of days after this picture was taken, the stranglehold of the mighty *King* Class 4-6-0's was to be broken forever on the Birkenhead to Paddington route. With steam leaking from places it should not have, No 6015 *King Richard III* (84A Wolverhampton - Stafford Road) throws a pall of smoke high into the sky as it accelerated an up express through Monmore Green (Priestfield) on 7th September 1962. (T. R. Amos)

71) Complete with a rake of chocolate and cream coaches and headboard, a pristine *Castle* Class 4-6-0 No 7035 *Ogmore Castle*, from 85B Gloucester (Horton Road) picks up speed through Swindon, after coming off the Gloucester line with the Paddington bound *Cheltenham Spa Express* in May 1960. *Ogmore Castle* was not long fresh from overhaul at Swindon Works, where it had received a double chimney in January of the same year. (N. E. Preedy)

72)   9400 Class 0-6-0PT No 8459, from 86G Pontypool Road, struggles up the incline from Llanhilleth to Crumlin High Level Junction, with a goods train on a misty 14th October 1963. Assistance from the rear was being provided by 5600 Class 0-6-2T No 6634, a stablemate of 8495 at Pontypool Road. Llanhilleth station had closed completely in 1962. (W. Potter)

73)   5101 Class 2-6-2T No 5190 awaits workshop attention at its home depot at 84E Tyseley on 22nd May 1949. This locomotive, which was constructed at Swindon in 1934, was carrying the standard B.R. mixed traffic livery with the plain cream lettering of BRITISH RAILWAYS on the side tanks. 5190 was made surplus to requirements in September 1962, being withdrawn from 83C Exeter (St. Davids), being cut up thirteen months later (A. N. H. Glover)

74)   Former Taff Railway 'A' Class 0-6-2T No 309, in ex. works condition on shed at 88A Cardiff (Cathays) on 19th June 1949.
A Cameron design of 1912, they consisted of fifty-eight engines, forming the T.V's largest class. They were re-boilered
by the GWR, following grouping and were highly successful in their rebuilt form. All fifty-eight members survived when
taken over by B.R. and 309 lasted until 1953. (A. N. H. Glover)

75)   During the last couple of years or so of Western Region steam, the authorities had given up all pretence of cleanliness
with the surviving steam fleet. By 1965 this attitude had spread to most other regions as can be seen by this dreadful
example of a London Midland based BR Class 9F 2-10-0 No 92218 (2D Banbury) seen at Oxford in November 1965 at
the head of a coal train. Surprisingly, 92218 stayed in service until May 1968. (G. W. Sharpe)

76) With steam leaking from the cylinders, *Hall* Class 4-6-0 No 5990 *Dorford Hall*, from 84C Banbury, was noted at speed on an unidentified express working at Didcot on 4th April 1963. For many years an occupant of 87E Landore, *Dorford Hall* had been transferred to Banbury in March 1960. It was to remain there until condemned in January 1965, being cut up on site by Friswells Ltd., five months later. (Ken Ellis)

77) A variety of enthusiasts wander up and down the remote tracks at Serridge Junction after being disgorged from the 'Severn Venturer' train on 15th April 1956, which was being hauled by 1600 Class 0-6-0PT No 1625, a Gloucester engine. 1625 had propelled the train onto the Lydbrook branch, for running round, before returning to Lydney. The station at Serridge Junction had closed as early as 1879. (F. Hornby)

78) 5700 Class 0-6-0PT No 9732 outside the repair shop at the vast depot of 86A Newport (Ebbw Junction) on 12th June 1949. The angle of the camera 'suggests' that the cab roof of 9732 is adorned with its own special lighting arrangements!!! Ebbw Junction, in common with some other major Western Region depots, had a traverser at the entrance to the repair shop, the easiest and cheapest method of filling the many roads inside. (B. W. L. Brooksbank)

79) Two 'Earls' stand side by side at the entrance to 84G Shrewsbury shed in October 1961. *Castle* Class 4-6-0's Nos 5048 *Earl of Devon* (88A Cardiff - Canton) and 5059 *Earl St. Aldwyn*, a Shrewsbury engine, both in good external condition await their next duties. Both were early victims of modernisation, 5048 being withdrawn in August 1962, from 87F Llanelly and 5059 from Shrewsbury two months earlier. (G. W. Sharpe)

80) Maximum effort at Plymouth (North Road) on 16th August 1958. *Hall* Class 4-6-0 No 4967 *Shirenewton Hall* (83A Newton Abbot) pilots *Modified Hall* Class 4-6-0 No 6991 *Acton Burnell Hall* (81C Southall) as they surge out of North Road station with the up *Royal Duchy*, bound for Paddington. The use of two mixed traffic locomotives on this train suggests a shortage of *Castles* and *Kings* on this date. Note that the train engine is carrying the headboard as opposed to the leading locomotive. (Terry Nicholls)

81) With the weeds gradually taking over the platform and tracks, 6400 Class 0-6-0PT No 6403, from 86G Pontypool Road, pauses at the former London & North Western terminus at Ebbw Vale High Level with a Stephenson Locomotive Society special on a rain-soaked and thoroughly miserable 11th July 1953. The station at Ebbw Vale High Level had closed in 1951, with the Western Region Low Level station following suit eleven years later. (F. Hornby)

82) Two local inmates of 81B Slough stand outside the four track depot on 26th March 1961. Nearest the camera is 9400 Class 0-6-0PT No 9415 with 6100 Class 2-6-2T No 6143 in attendance. 6143 was to remain allocated to Slough until the shed demised in June 1964. 9415, however, had moved on to pastures new, at 81C Southall in August 1962. Both engines continued working well into 1965. (A. N. H. Glover)

83)   There were always lines of locomotives out in the open on various tracks within the confines of 87D Swansea East Dock shed right up until the closure of the shed on 13th June 1964. Photographed in the yard on 7th June 1953 were three resident engines – 4200 Class 2-8-0 Tanks Nos 4283 and 4259, with 5700 Class 0-6-0PT No 7756 completing the trio. After closure, the shed was used for the storage of withdrawn engines. (F. Hornby)

84)   Man against machine at Kingswear in the summer of 1960. The driver of *County* Class 4-6-0 No 1007 *County of Brecknock*, struggles to rotate his charge on the turntable, the pit of which is completely overgrown with weeds. Once turned, *County of Brecknock*, with express lamps already in place, would be ready for a return journey to its home depot at 83C Exeter (St. Davids). 1007 was equipped with a double chimney in May 1957. (D. K. Jones)

85)   *Modified Hall* Class 4-6-0 No 6973 *Bricklehampton Hall*, allocated to 88A Cardiff East Dock, dwarfs the London underground stock as it passed through Ealing broadway station, just under six miles away from Paddington, with an up South Wales to Acton Yard fitted freight on 19th October 1963. Between July 1964 and withdrawal in August 1965, 6973 served at 87A Neath, 86E Severn Tunnel Junction and 82E Bristol (Barrow Road). (J. K. Carter)

86)   It was not often that locomotives of similar numerical sequence were photographed together. This picture captures just that coincidence at Aberbeeg on 22nd October 1962. The signalbox at Aberbeeg towers over 9400 Class 0-6-0 Pannier Tanks Nos 8444 (leading) and 9444 which were awaiting banking duties. Both engines were based at the nearby local shed, coded 86F. (W. Potter)

87) A heavy downpour of rain greets the arrival of 4300 Class 2-6-0 No 7333 (83B Taunton) as it steamed into the platform at Dulverton with a local passenger from Taunton to Barnstaple on 21st April 1962. Waiting in another platform, with steam to spare, is 5700 Class 0-6-0PT No 3659 (83C Exeter - St. Davids) with an Exe Valley train bound for Exeter. Dulverton station died for ever during 1966. (Terry Nicholls)

88) In true 'Thomas the Tank' style, the open doors of the diminutive narrow gauge shed of the Vale of Rheidol, reveal the presence of one of the delightful V of R Tanks No 8 *Llywelyn* undergoing maintenance in June 1962. In more recent years the former standard gauge shed at Aberystwyth was taken over by *Llywelyn* and sister engines No 7 *Owain Glyndwr* and No 9 *Prince of Wales*. (N. L. Browne)

89)	With heaps of discarded ash in the foreground, 1500 Class 0-6-0PT No 1505 simmers on the coaling stage road at its home shed of 81A Old Oak Common on 10th April 1957, in company with an unidentified 5700 Class 0-6-0PT of the 9700 series, fitted with condensing apparatus. 1505 remained at Old Oak Common until condemned in May 1962. It was scrapped at Wolverhampton Works the following month. (N. L. Browne)

90)	When someone pulls the wrong points lever at the wrong time we have what can be loosely described as a mishap. Parted from its tender and derailed at Parson Street Junction on 12th September 1963 was BR Class 9F 2-10-0 No 92243 (88A Cardiff East Dock). *Modified Hall* Class 4-6-0 No 7907 *Hart Hall* (82B St. Philip's Marsh), its crew agog with curiosity, crawls past the unfortunate 92243 with a down passenger train. (Terry Nicholls)

91) With its tender fully laden with fresh coal supplies, *County* Class 4-6-0 No 1008 *County of Cardigan* (84K Chester) had been stopped temporarily as the 'Not to be Moved' sign on the front bufferbeam suggests. *County of Cardigan* was a visitor to 86C Cardiff (Canton) on 13th September 1953. A double chimney was fitted to this engine in May 1958. (N. E. Preedy)

92) With a full head of steam, 4500 Class 2-6-2T No 5518, from 85B Gloucester (Horton Road), departs, bunker-first, from Churchdown with a passenger train from Cheltenham to Gloucester and Paddington on 30th October 1963. Sister engine No 4564 was also based at Horton Road at this stage in time. 5518 was withdrawn in May 1964 with 4564 following on four months later. Churchdown station also demised in 1964. (P. A. Rowlings)

93)   Banbury was a cosmopolitan meeting place which not only had the main line traffic from Paddington, Oxford and Birmingham with its great variety of locomotive classes but also there were a number of trains from the ex. Great Central line, to and from Woodford and beyond to be seen. On 21st May 1960, LNER L1 Class 2-6-4T No 67743, based at 2F Woodford Halse, was ready for departure with a local to Woodford. (N. L. Browne)

94)   Towards the end of April 1964, the once extremely busy shed at 82B St. Philip's Marsh, was in the latter stages of being run down prior to complete closure on 14th June 1964. On 27th April 1964 an equally run down member of the *Grange* Class 4-6-0's No 6867 *Peterston Grange*, a visitor to 'Spam' from 87A Neath, was all but on its own inside the almost derelict twin roundhouse. (D. K. Jones)

95)   In a flurry of white steam, soot-stained *Hall* Class 4-6-0 No 4988 *Bulwell Hall*, a Welsh engine from 87F Llanelly, hurries an excursion through the splendid gardens at Bath in the early afternoon of 10th August 1963. The following month, *Bulwell Hall* was drafted to 81F Oxford from where it was condemned in February 1964. Oblivion for 4988 came a month later in the cutting up shop at Swindon Works. (R. Picton)

96)   Deep in the heart of Cornwall, at Truro, in the summer of 1952, *County* Class 4-6-0 No 1015 *County of Gloucester*, an 83D Laira (Plymouth) engine, sets off with the Penzance to Plymouth leg of the up *Cornish Riviera* express, the premier Western Region train. *County of Gloucester* was withdrawn from Laira in December 1962 but was not scrapped until May 1964, at Cashmores, Newport. (John Smith)

97)   In true British Railways fashion a member of the station staff at Dudley takes things easy by leaning against a short signal post on 31st August 1959. It was a good job that the signal arm was not much longer or our friend might have been enjoying an enforced sleep on the platform, if the signal had dropped down!!! 6400 Class 0-6-0PT No 6422 (84A Wolverhampton - Stafford Road) was being employed on a parcels train. (T. R. Amos)

98)   'Reflections' at Pontsticill Junction on 26th May 1956. As a two coach auto-train from Merthyr Tydfil was being pushed into the station it was captured on film by the photographer from his train which was departing to Newport. Why the auto-train, being pushed by 6400 Class 0-6-0PT No 6413 (86J Aberdare) was allowed into the station before the Newport train cleared the next home signal is a mystery. (N. L. Browne)

99)   Time to drop the fire in the yard at 88E Abercynon on 12th August 1964 for 5600 Class 0-6-2T No 6685 after it returned
        to its home shed having completed its days work. Note the stencilled shed-code on the smokebox. Soon the fire in 6685
        will be dropped for the final time with withdrawal only one month away. The cold and lifeless hulk of 6685 was stored
        at Abercynon until December 1964, whence it was dragged to Newport for scrapping by Cashmores. (D. K. Jones)

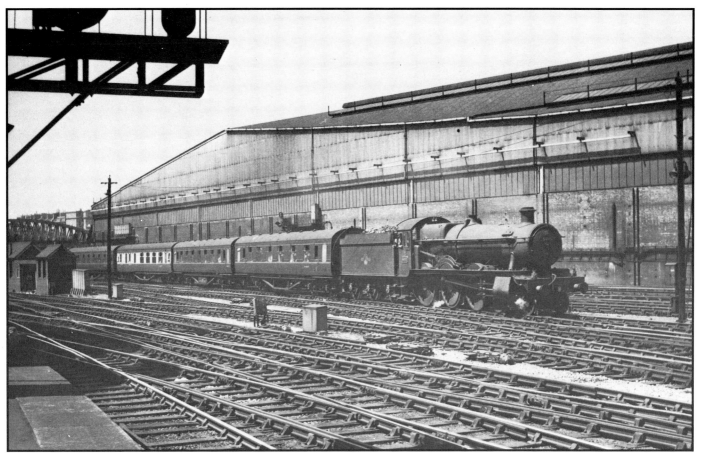

100) Arrival time at Paddington on 4th July 1959. *Hall* Class 4-6-0 No 5996 *Mytton Hall*, from 81C Southall, takes a centre road amidst the mass of trackwork as it moved serenely into the station with an up express, consisting of London Midland Region stock. From 1959 onwards more and more expresses to and from Paddington, especially to the West Country, were taken over by the ever increasing numbers of main line diesels. (F. Hornby)

101) Dowlais Central station on 21st May 1955 where a bunker-first 5600 Class 0-6-0PT No 5605 (88D Merthyr) was reversing its two coach through train from Bargoed. Dowlais, in the heart of the Welsh Valley's had no less than seven stations at different stages in time, these being at Dowlais (Taff Vale), Cae Harris, Central, High Street, Junction, Top (Brecon & Merthyr) & Top (LNW). Central itself closed in 1960. (N. L. Browne)

102) The Western station at Exeter (St. Davids) hosted many trains of Southern origins and Southern locomotives were frequent visitors. Southern trains bound for destinations like Barnstaple and Okehampton gained access to these routes via St. Davids and Cowley Bridge Junction. Arriving at St. Davids on 9th July 1956 with a passenger from the Okehampton direction was SR 'Greyhound' T9 Class 4-4-0 No 30711 (72A Exmouth Junction). (F. Hornby)

103) Stroud Central station in the heart of the Cotswolds on a cold 24th February 1962. Black smoke is churned out of the funnel of 1400 Class 0-4-2T No 1424, from 85B Gloucester (Horton Road), as it readied itself for departure with a push and pull auto-train from Chalford to Gloucester. The former Midland Railway station at Stroud had closed as early as 1947. 1424 continued working from Horton Road until condemned in November 1963. (B. W. L. Brooksbank)

104) Pontypool Road, situated between Abergavenny and Newport (Monmouth), had a large engine shed, coded 86G. It was one of those tantalising places which used to frustrate spotters who were on trains passing the depot. It was always difficult to know which numbers to write down before the shed disappeared into the distance. The yard and shed was photographed from the cab of GWR Railcar No W13 on 27th May 1956. (F. Hornby)

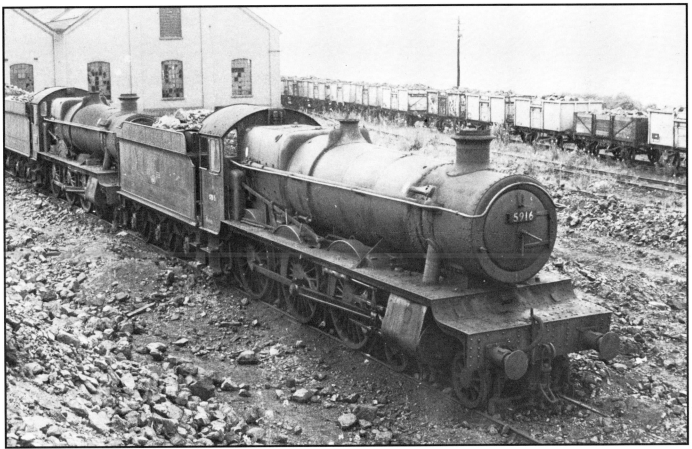

105) The large twin roundhouses at 84B Oxley (Wolverhampton) used to supply steam engines for the more secondary express workings along with the bulk of freight trains to and from the area and constantly lived in the shadow of its more illustrious neighbour at Stafford Road (84A) until the latter closed in September 1963. In store on a back road on 29th July 1962 was a condemned *Hall* Class 4-6-0 No 5916 *Trinity Hall*. (B. G. Price)

106) By the summer of 1960 all of the lines associated with the former Somerset & Dorset lines were firmly in the grip of the Western Region. Little had changed in terms of the motive power employed on these routes, with examples from the GWR, LMR, SR and BR classes to be seen on a regular basis. Ex. Midland Railway designed Class 2P 4-4-0 No 40696, from 82F Bath Green Park runs round its train at Templecombe. (A. C. Ingram)

107) A nicely spruced up BR Class 4 4-6-0 No 75028, allocated to 6E Chester (West) enters Bala Junction on 11th June 1959 with the four coach 12.45 pm Pwllheli to Chester local passenger train. The lines veering off to the right of 75028 led to Blaenau Festiniog, now long since lifted. The station at Bala Junction, situated in a rather remote part of Wales, closed in 1956. (B. W. L. Brooksbank)

108)   The meek and the mighty at 83D Laira (Plymouth) in 1959. An unidentified 5700 Class 0-6-0PT is dwarfed by *King* Class
4-6-0 No 6025 *King Henry III*, a resident of Laira, near to the coaling plant after arrival at the shed having hauled the
9.30 am express from Paddington. Above *King Henry III*, 5700 Class 0-6-0PT No 3787 finds employment shunting coal
wagons. Like 6025, 3787 also belonged to Laira. (R. W. Hinton)

109)   The weekend of 8th/9th September was the last for regular rostered steam haulage of expresses on the Paddington to
Birmingham (Snow Hill) and Wolverhampton (Low Level) route. On Saturday 8th September 1962, *Castle* Class 4-6-0
No 5046 *Earl Cawdor*, an 84A Wolverhampton (Stafford Road) sped through Greenford with the up *Cambrian Coast
Express*, devoid of any headboard. *Earl Cawdor* was withdrawn the following day. (R. Picton)

110) After having traversed the bridge over the river Usk and passed the remains of Newport Castle, WD Class 8F 2-8-0 No 90672 takes a down centre track through Newport (High Street) and heads towards Cardiff with a Class 8 loose-coupled freight on 5th June 1961. 90672 would provide some spotters with a rare 'cop' being shedded at the far away depot of 2F Woodford Halse, in former Great Central territory. (B. W. L. Brooksbank)

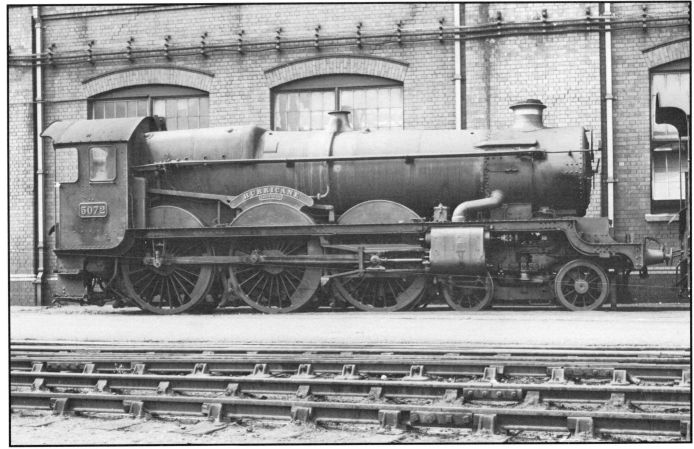

111) *Castle* Class 4-6-0 No 5072 *Hurricane*, allocated to 87E Landore, disconnected from its tender, awaits attention outside Swindon Works 'A' shop on 14th June 1953. The main Great Western workshops were established at Swindon in 1840 and eventually became one of the largest and most up to date plants, for repairs and construction of locomotives, carriages and wagons anywhere in the world and covered an area of 323 acres. (A. N. H. Glover)

112) Collett and Hawksworth passenger locomotives side by side in front of the running shed at 87E Landore (Swansea) in September 1954. Nearest to the camera, paired with a straight-sided tender, is *Castle* Class 4-6-0 No 7018 *Drysllwyn Castle* in company with *County* Class 4-6-0 No 1000 *County of Middlesex*. *Drysllwyn Castle* was later fitted with a double chimney, in May 1956. (L. Brownhill)

113) With its boiler casing marked by months of graft and neglect, BR Class 9F 2-10-0 No 92128, from the former GWR shed at Banbury but now owned by the LMR (2D), approaches Tramway Crossing, Gloucester on 19th June 1965 with a Banbury to South Wales iron ore train. 92128 was transferred to 2E Saltley upon closure of Banbury in late 1966 and ended its working days at 10A Carnforth, being made redundant in November 1967. (N. E. Preedy)

114) A group of young locospotters are gathered on the station footbridge at Barmouth on an unspecified day in 1960. The road ahead is clear for *Manor* Class 4-6-0 No 7820 *Dinmore Manor* at the head of a goods train. The lines around Barmouth were amongst the most famous haunts for these popular mixed traffic engines. *Dinmore Manor* was withdrawn from 6D Shrewsbury in November 1965 and is now preserved. (Kit Windle)

115) The driver of 83C Exeter (St. Davids) based 5101 Class 2-6-2T No 4117, in excellent external condition, stands by the cab of his charge as it replenishes its water supplies in the yard at 83A Newton Abbot on 12th July 1958. The angle of the camera suggests that the fireman of 4117 is sitting astride the safety valve cover!!! Next to 4117 is a locally based sister engine in the shape of 5153. (A. Swain)

116) Yet another engine taking on water supplies. The fireman of a resplendent *Modified Hall* Class 4-6-0 No 6994 *Baggrave Hall*, from 82D Westbury, supervises the flow of water from his lofty viewpoint on the tender, in the shed yard at 82F Weymouth on 22nd May 1957. *Baggrave Hall* remained at Westbury until October 1961, serving at 83C Exeter (St. Davids), 81C Southall, 89A Shrewsbury and 2B Oxley before withdrawal in November 1964. (A. N. H. Glover)

117) The young fireman of WD Class 8F 2-8-0 No 90693, based at 86C Cardiff (Canton), looks towards the camera from the cab of the same whilst standing, light engine, on a through road at Oxford on 21st May 1960. Note the numberplate was set in a higher position on the smokebox than most other members of the class. Transferred to 84C Banbury in January 1961, 90693 ended its days at 81C Southall in October 1962. (N. L. Browne)

118) Splendid close-up photographs like this one appear very rarely for one reason or another. One can almost hear the conversations of the footplate crew and the sing of the injector as 4300 Class 2-6-0 No 5358 (82D Westbury) stood at its namesake station – circa 1959. Apart from the normal parts associated with the footplate, there is a 'billy can' of tea being kept warm above the firebox door and a clean rag for the benefit of the crew is slung over the whistle chain. 5358 was withdrawn from service in July 1962. (M. F. Higson)

119) Nearly thirty years ago the BR *Britannia* Class 4-6-2's allocated to 86C Cardiff (Canton) were still the pride and joy of the depot. More often than not they were to be found at the head of crack expresses like the *Capitals United* and the *Red Dragon*. At speed, in charge of the former express, near Patchway on 10th September 1960 was No 70019 *Lightning*, in good condition, complete with headboard and reporting number. (R. Picton)

120) Former Midland Railway Class 3F 0-6-0 No 43436, shedded at 82G Templecombe, was photographed from a passing train, whilst shunting the ex. Somerset & Dorset Railway works yard at Highbridge on a dull day in 1958. 43436 had a complete change of scene in July 1961, being despatched to the London Midland Region and being based at 24B Rose Grove until condemned in June 1962. It was cut up at the Central Wagon Co., Wigan. (A. C. Ingram)

121) LMS Class 5 4-6-0 No 45298, paired with a self-weighing tender, was photographed near to the locoshed at Shrewsbury in 1962 at the head of an empty stock train. This engine was a particular favourite of Shrewsbury shed and had been based there for many years. It was transferred, presumably rather reluctantly, away to 6H Bangor in June 1964. In June 1967 45298 was at its last home, 5B Crewe (South) – withdrawn in September. (N. E. Preedy)

122) BR *Britannia* Class 4-6-2 No 70052 *Firth of Tay* (5A Crewe - North), in appalling external condition, blackens the skyline as it attacked the bank at Bradenham, near West Wycombe, with a returning F.A. Cup Final special from Wembley to Preston, filled with disconsolate Preston North End football supporters on 2nd May 1964. Built in 1954, *Firth of Tay* was paired with a larger capacity high sided tender. (D. Coles)

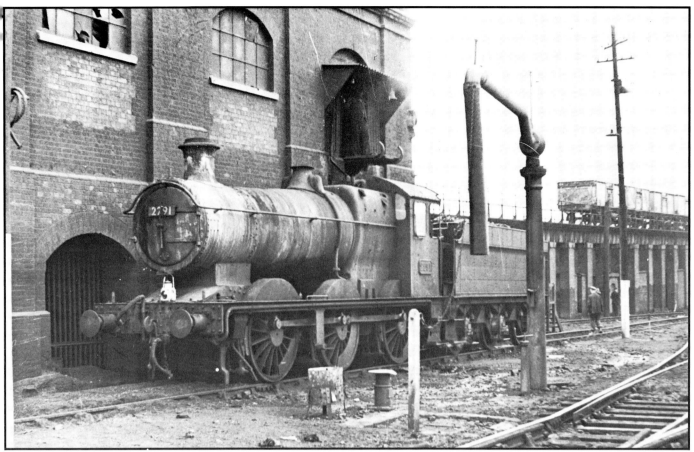

123) A more than grubby Collett 2251 Class 0-6-0 No 2291 is matched by its surroundings as it was being supplied with coal from the primitive coaler at 82C Swindon on 28th April 1963. 2291, a Swindon engine, was despatched to 85A Worcester in January 1964 and condemned eight months later. The 28th April 1963 was a sad date in time with the final run of a *King* Class 4-6-0 in public service – 6018 *King Henry VI* – Birmingham to Swindon and return. (B. G. Price)

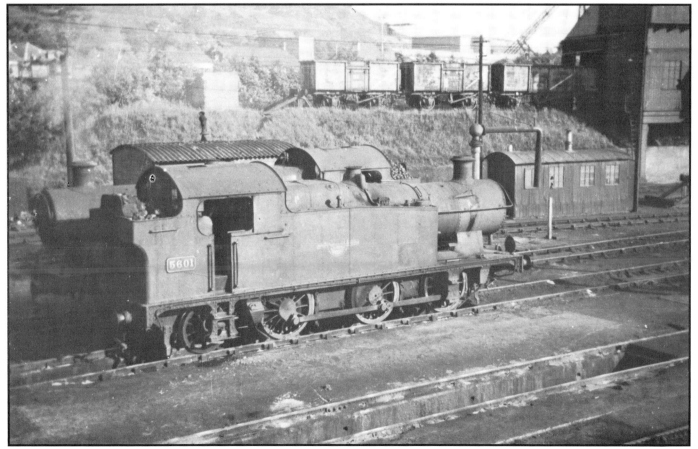

124) For many a year the 5600 Class 0-6-2 Tanks became part of the every-day railway scenery in South Wales until their demise in this part of the world in mid 1965. On 15th May 1963, a locally based 5601 prepared to leave the yard at 88E Abercynon for a freight duty. Abercynon shed, opened by the GWR in 1929, closed completely on 2nd November 1964. Upon closure 5601 moved to 88D Rhymney but was withdrawn two months later. (D. K. Jones)

125) Steam triumphs over diesel power at Reading on 31st August 1963. An 81D Reading *Manor* Class 4-6-0 No 7817 *Garsington Manor* had been commandeered to assist an ailing 'Hymeck' further down the line. Upon arrival at Reading a large crowd had gathered to observe the humiliation of the 'Hymeck' being removed from the express it was previously hauling, by a triumphant *Garsington Manor*. Note the unusual array of semaphore signals. (D. Oakes)

126) Refuelled and almost ready for the next duty, *Hall* Class 4-6-0 No 5904 *Kelham Hall*, from 82B St. Philip's Marsh, had its smokebox door fully open outside the straight shed at 86E Severn Tunnel Junction on an unknown day in 1961. Judging by the position of the lengthy ladder behind *Kelham Hall* an attempt was being made to replace some of the loose and missing tiles on the roof of the shed building. (T. Walker)

127) A rather wet and generally miserable day on 12th June 1964 greets the arrival of 5700 Class 0-6-0PT No 3717 (86G Pontypool Road) as it drew into Hafodyrnys Platform with a two coach local passenger train from Pontypool Road to Neath. 3717 a longstanding inmate of Pontypool Road remained there until May 1965 but was withdrawn the following month from 88B Cardiff (Radyr). Hafodyrynys Platform closed during 1964. (W. Potter)

128) The summer services in 1965 provided some of the surviving ex. Great Western passenger engines with last opportunities to perform on express duties, albeit in the main on excursion traffic. An absolutely filthy *Hall* Class 4-6-0 No 6918 *Sandon Hall* (82E Bristol - Barrow Road) was photographed, minus name and cab numberplates, at Lawrence Hill, Bristol with a holiday extra on 31st July 1965. (B. W. L. Brooksbank)

129) 5400 Class 0-6-0PT No 5420, an inhabitant of the nearby 85B Gloucester (Horton Road), finds itself dumped on a remote siding at 85C Gloucester (Barnwood) early in 1962 in company with two unidentified LMS Class 3F 'Jinty' 0-6-0 Tanks. 1963 was to be a strange year for 5420 – transferred to Barnwood in July, it was sent to 72C Yeovil the following month and returned to Barnwood the month after and was withdrawn in October. (P. A. Rowlings)

130) A young spotter stares in awe at *Castle* Class 4-6-0 No 5025 *Chirk Castle*, an 81F Oxford engine as it accelerated a down express out of Birmingham (Snow Hill and headed for Hockley and beyond on 20th January 1962. Waiting for a path out of Snow Hill at the same time was 7400 Class 0-6-0PT No 7426 (84E Tyseley) once a resident of 86E Severn Tunnel Junction, 85C Hereford and 84F Stourbridge sheds. (P. A. Rowlings)

131) Dazzling sunshine reflects off the platform at Evercreech Junction on the old Somerset & Dorset Railway on 22nd July 1964. A begrimed 82F Bath Green Park BR Class 5 4-6-0 No 73049 had paused at the station with the 9.53 am passenger train from Bath Green Park to Bournemouth. Two months later and 73049 was drafted to its last home at 81F Oxford, being made surplus to requirements in March 1965. (H. L. Holland)

132) Very few British steam locomotives were ever equipped with the ugly American style of spark arresters, thank goodness, as they did nothing whatsoever to enhance their general appearance. Steam issued defiantly from the safety valves of a home based 1600 Class 0-6-0PT No 1661 as it stood outside the shed at 85A Worcester in the early spring of 1962. 1661, complete with a home-made front numberplate had been unofficially named *Vinegar Castle*. (P. A. Rowlings)

133) A dull and overcast day at Crumlin High Level on 27th May 1956 where 7200 Class 2-8-2T No 7201 had paused briefly to enable the driver to hand over the single line token to the signalman, after traversing Crumlin Viaduct. 7201 was allocated to 86G Pontypool Road, a depot it was to remain at until July 1964. Crumlin High Level station closed in 1964, two years after the Low Level station had finished serving the local community. (N. L. Browne)

134) An immense row of brick built terraced houses gaze down upon Senghenydd station, terminus of the short branch line from Aber on 21st May 1955. Most of the platform had been taken over by nature creating a 'field' within its confines. 4500 Class 2-6-2T No 5568 (88A Cardiff - Cathays) awaited departure with a local train bound for Cardiff (Queen Street). Senghenydd station, of Rhymney Railway origin, was another victim of the 1964 closure plan. (N. L. Browne)

135) Having negotiated the gradient on the approaches to Bodmin Road station in Cornwall, *Hall* Class 4-6-0 No 5975 *Winslow Hall*, allocation unknown, glides into the station with a Penzance to Plymouth express on 5th July 1955. The line in the right of the picture led to Bodmin (GWR) and Wadebridge. Both the former Great Western and Southern Railway stations at Bodmin were closed in 1967. (D. K. Jones)

136) A rather less than immaculate *Castle* Class 4-6-0 No 5096 *Bridgwater Castle*, from 88A Cardiff (Canton) draws into Newport (High Street) with the 6.20 pm express to Paddington on 3rd June 1962. *Bridgwater Castle*, seen here matched with a straight-sided tender, was sent to the newly re-opened shed at Cardiff East Dock in September 1962 when Canton closed its doors to steam. It was condemned in 1964, from 85A Worcester. (R. Picton)

137)	The powerhouse workhorses in the freight world of the Western region, were the Churchward 2800 Class 2-8-0's. No 2841 (81D Reading) fills thc air with smoke and steam as it runs briskly through Swindon on a centre track with a mixed goods on Saturday, 30th September 1961. Only a few of the 2800 series survived until 1965, basically the end of steam on the Western Region but a large number of the more modern 3800 series did. 2841 was withdrawn from 81C Southall in December 1963. (J. D. Gomersall)

138) A disgustingly filthy *County* Class 4-6-0 No 1028 *County of Warwick*, not exactly a good advert for British Railways, enters Severn Tunnel Junction station with a relief express bound for Paignton from the Cardiff direction on 28th July 1962. Despite sporting an 82A Bristol (Bath Road) shedplate, *County of Warwick* was allocated to 82B St. Philip's Marsh, as Bath Road had closed to steam in September 1960. (R. Picton)

139) We remain in Wales and move westwards to Whitland, on the borders of what was then Carmarthenshire and Pembrokeshire, before they changed to the names they now have, which few folk outside of Wales can relate to. Outside the small sub-shed in June 1963 were 6100 Class 2-6-2T No 6118 and 4500 Class 2-6-2T No 5508, both from 87H Neyland. Next to the shed is a train of large pipes, probably for the oil industry. (N. L. Browne)

140) A nice sunny day at Minehead, in Somerset in July 1960, where 2251 Class 0-6-0 No 2277, from 83B Taunton, was shunting the branch goods train. 2277 had been transferred to Taunton from 82B St. Philip's Marsh, the previous month. Minehead station was closed by British Railways in 1971 but is now an important part of the preservation scene, in the safe hands of the West Somerset Railway. (R. S. Carpenter)

141) The lamps on the bufferbeam of *Hall* Class 4-6-0 No 5918 *Walton Hall*, are nice and clean, which is more than can be said of the locomotive. There is a nicc display of Great Western signals, as *Walton Hall*, from 81F Oxford, drifted into Castle Cary with a parcels train on 11th November 1961. Despite the state of the engine, 5918 was to soldier on in revenue earning service until September 1962. Scrapping came at King's, Norwich. (Peter Hay)

142)   A partial view of one of the two roundhouses at 87F Llanelly on 7th April 1958. Facing the camera, from left to right are: 7200 Class 2-8-2T No 7211, 1600 Class 0-6-0PT No 1633, 5700 Class 0-6-0PT No 3642, 1600 Class 0-6-0PT No 1607 and 5700 Class 0-6-0PT No 5722. All of these engines were on Llanelly's books. The shed was opened in 1925, replacing the original depot which was built in 1840. (B. W. L. Brooksbank)

143)   A plume of smoke pours from the chimney of *Castle* Class 4-6-0 No 5040 *Stokesay Castle*, whilst it was being topped up with coal, a dirty thankless task, at 81A Old Oak Common on 10th April 1957. *Stokesay Castle* remained allocated to Old Oak Common until October 1961, when it became the property of 82B St. Philip's Marsh until withdrawn in October 1963. Scrapping came at Coopers Metals, Sharpness in May 1964. (N. L. Browne)

144)   A bedraggled looking 4300 Class 2-6-0 No 6347 in the yard of its home shed at 87G Carmarthen on 22nd April 1962.
Records show that 6347 was at 87H Neyland in January 1957, moving on to 87J Goodwick in October 1957, on to
Carmarthen in May 1960, then back to Neyland in June 1961, returning to Carmarthen three months later and finally
to 87F Llanelly in June 1962, where it died in December 1963. (R. Picton)

145)   A fine panoramic view of BR Class 9F 2-10-0 No 92224 (2D Banbury), hard at work near to Stoke Orchard, north of
Cheltenham, on the Bristol to Birmingham main linc, with a northbound freight on 30th July 1965. 92224 was constructed
in 1958 and served from Banbury (twice), 83D Laira (Plymouth), 81C Southall, 81F Oxford, 82F Bath Green Park, 82E
Bristol (Barrow Road), 88A Cardiff East Dock & 8B Warrington before withdrawal in September 1967. (K. L. Seal)

146) With a flurry of white exhaust showing, *Castle* Class 4-6-0 No 5075 *Wellington*, from 83D Laira (Plymouth), attacks Rattery bank, soon after passing Totnes, with the down *Royal Duchy* express, consisting of seven coaches, on 26th June 1958. The *Royal Duchy* was slightly in excess of 200 miles away from the starting point at Paddington. Rattery bank provided a stiff test for both engines and crews, being 1 in 46 at its worst. (J. Head)

147) A soot-encrusted *Manor* Class 4-6-0 No 7824 *Iford Manor*, was a visitor to Aberystwyth shed on 18th July 1960, from 84E Tyseley, where it was noted simmering gently in the yard awaiting a return trip to Birmingham. The depot at Aberystwyth was a sub-shed of 89C Machynlleth and was located in the fork of lines which went to Carmarthen and Dovey Junction. The shed closed to standard gauge engines in April 1965. (R. Picton)

148) For many years LMS Class 3 2-6-2T No 40171 was based at 86K Tredegar, in the Welsh Valley's. In June 1960 it was transferred briefly to 82E Bristol (Barrow Road). Three months later 40171 found itself in former Somerset and Dorset territory at 82G Templecombe, where it was photographed out of steam on 11th September 1960. One final move in May 1961 took 40171 to 6A Chester, where it was condemned the same month. (A. N. H. Glover)

149) With a fine looking miniature lower quadrant signal gantry looking on, 5700 Class 0-6-0PT No 5798, from Taunton, coasts into Frome station with a rake of coaching stock in the summer of 1958. 5798 remained an ever present locomotive at Taunton until no longer required, being withdrawn from service in September 1962. It was stored at Taunton until December 1963, meeting its fate at Cashmores, Newport a month later. (A. C. Ingram)

150) Smartly turned out, with a nicely lined tender and cab, with the old *Lion & Wheel* logo on the tender, *Modified Hall* Class 4-6-0 No 7911 *Lady Margaret Hall*, draws into Birmingham (Snow Hill) with an up local passenger train, consisting of non-corridor stock – circa 1957. *Lady Margaret Hall*, a longstanding occupant of 81F Oxford, stayed in service there until condemnation arrived in December 1963. (R. S. Carpenter)

151) Sunlight and shadows within the lengthy confines of the running shed at 88F Treherbert in 1960. Most of the occupants are from the 5600 Class 0-6-2 Tanks and nearest to the camera is 5626, a visitor from 88D Merthyr, with a smartly painted front numberplate. On the adjacent track next to 5626, is 5613, a Treherbert engine. Built in 1931, 88F closed completely on 1st March 1965. (D. K. Jones)

152) Based at the near at hand shed (87F), 5700 Class 0-6-0PT No 8785 was shunting carriages at Llanelly station on 26th May 1956. In the background, another 0-6-0 Pannier Tank can be observed. 8785 remained at 87F Llanelly until condemned in December 1963. It lay rotting in store for two months before being towed away for cutting up at Birds, Morriston, Swansea in March 1964. (N. L. Browne)

153) In the shadow of a huge gasometer, an ex.works Churchward 4300 Class 2-6-0 No 6351, a visitor to 84C Banbury, from 82B St. Philip's Marsh, was in the process of having its fire cleaned in August 1959. To the right of 6351 is a breakdown crane. 6351, a loyal servant of St. Philip's Marsh, for many years, was discarded by 'Spam' in November 1960 and scrapped at Swindon in February 1961. (L. C. Jacks)

154)   A scorching hot day at 83G Penzance on 24th June 1951, three and a half years after nationalisation. Weeds sprout healthily amongst the trackwork in the foreground, whilst in the left of the picture, a stream of water leaks from the hose of a water column. The main focus of attention is *Hall* Class 4-6-0 No 6931 *Aldborough Hall*, allocation not known, in company with an unidentified *Modified Hall* Class 4-6-0. (R. S. Carpenter)

155)   Two coaches and a van make up the load for 2251 Class 0-6-0 No 2219 (83B Taunton)) as it left Evercreech Junction (S. & D.) with the lunch-time passenger train to Highbridge and Burnham-on-Sea, on a cold and wet 11th November 1961. By this date, the old enemy of the S. & D., in the shape of GWR engines and coaches had gained a foothold but it only lasted less than five more years. (Peter Hay)

156)   Travelling light engine, *Modified Hall* Class 4-6-0 No 6982 *Melmerby Hall*, yet another 82B St. Philip's Marsh engine, speeds past Northfield Foot Crossing between Gloucester and Bristol, on 23rd October 1963. With the distant at caution, the progress homewards for *Melmerby Hall*, may well have been hampered by the next signal being at danger. 6982 was transferred to 82E Bristol (Barrow Road) upon closure of 82B in June 1964 but was withdrawn two months later. (N. E. Preedy)

157)   84C Banbury based *Hall* Class 4-6-0 No 4964 *Rodwell Hall*, finds itself at the head of a local passenger train at Bristol (Temple Meads) on a sunny June day in 1959. Note the wooden station nameboard, which was a common feature of the GWR and later the Western Region of British Railways. *Rodwell Hall* was drafted to 84A Wolverhampton (Stafford Road) in July 1962 and to 86G Pontypool Road, its final home, two months later. (H. H. Bleads)

158)   4500 Class 2-6-2T No 5560 (86F Tondu) with a local passenger train, consisting of two antiquated coaches, at Nantymoel, terminus of the branch line from Tondu, on 14th August 1954. The line closed in 1958 as did Nantymoel and the intermediate stations of Wyndham Halt, Ogmore Vale, Blackmill and Brynmenyn. One other station which once existed was Lewistown Halt, between Ogmore Vale and Blackmill, which closed in 1951. (N. L. Browne)

159) *Castle* Class 4-6-0 No 4094 *Dynevor Castle*, speeds along level track in spartan and flat countryside at Westerleigh with an unknown express working on 6th September 1958. The white buffers are a give-a-way as to where *Dynevor Castle* was allocated to – 87E Landore (Swansea). It moved to 87F Llanelly in June 1961, when Landore was closed for rebuilding into a diesel depot. (D. K. Jones)

160) The 1500 Class 0-6-0 Pannier Tanks, introduced in 1949, were designed for heavy shunting duties and numbered only ten engines in total. In the mid-fifties, four examples of the class were based in South Wales – 1506 and 1507 were at 86B Newport (Pill), 1508 at 86C Cardiff (Canton) and 1509 at 86A Newport (Ebbw Junction). One of the duet allocated to Newport (Pill), 1506, was noted there on 27th May 1956. (N. L. Browne)

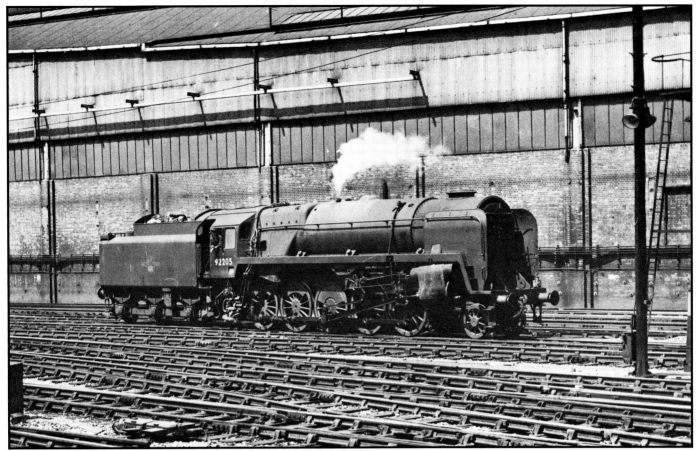

161) BR Class 9F 2-10-0's were quite often pressed into main line passenger services, particularly during the busy summer months, when there was a shortage of motive power. They were, however, rarely seen at Paddington, an exception being No 92205 (82B St. Philip's Marsh) on 4th July 1959. A gentle plume of steam trailed behind 92205 as it reversed slowly out of the station after arriving with an express from Paignton. (F. Hornby)

162) An impressive signal gantry, with its variety of lower semaphores, looks down upon the station scene at Shrewsbury on a bright October day in 1958. Sporting an express passenger headcode, 2251 Class 0-6-0 No 2289, a recent transfer to 84G Shrewsbury, gently drifts under the gantry with a solitary milk wagon which was to be attached to the coaches in the background. 2289 moved to 85B Gloucester (Horton Road) in October 1959. (N. E. Preedy)

163) Gaunt dwellings overlook the part of the shed yard at 82E Bristol (Barrow Road) which contained the coaling plant on an unspecified date in 1962. Between the main running lines in the right of the picture and the coaling plant is LMS Class 8F 2-8-0 No 48413, a visitor from 16B Kirkby. All but obscured in the right background is a locally based BR Class 9F 2-10-0 No 92248. (G. W. Sharpe)

164) The footplate crew of *Castle* Class 4-6-0 No 5042 *Winchester Castle* (87F Llanelly) brave the driving rain to pose for the camera, on a centre road at Carmarthen, with a three coach mail train on 6th June 1963. *Winchester Castle*, paired with a straight-sided tender, was destined to be one of the last working members of this famous class, being withdrawn from 85B Gloucester (Horton Road) in June 1965. (F. Hornby)

165) An immaculate SR E1/R Class 0-6-2T No 32124 (72A Exmouth Junction) takes a breather in the sidings at Exeter (St. Davids) on 9th July 1956. Built at Brighton Works as E1 Class 0-6-0T *Bayonne* (Stroudley), 32124 was rebuilt by Maunsell in 1928 as an 0-6-2T, for work in Devon and Cornwall. It was taken out of service in January 1959 and reduced to a pile of scrap at Eastleigh Works, two months later. (F. Hornby)

166) After a light overhaul, 2800 Class 2-8-0 No 2842 (81D Reading) emerged from Swindon Works on 16th October 1960 with only the front end, chimney and frames having been painted. The motion of 2824 had been degreased and revamped and it had been supplied with bright new number and shedplates on the smokebox. 2842 was re-allocated to 81E Didcot in November 1961 and was condemned from there in September 1963. (F. Hornby)

167)   The small depot at Lydney, was constructed by the Severn & Wye Railway in 1868. From 1935 until closure in March 1964 it was a sub-shed of 85B Gloucester (Horton Road). On 15th June 1963 there was an air of impending doom about the place, with piles of discarded ash strewn about the depot. 5700 Class 0-6-0PT No 4629 stood out of steam by a brick built platform and inside the shed was sister engine No 3721, both from 85B. (F. Hornby)

168)   A smartly cleaned *Hall* Class 4-6-0 No 4928 *Gatacre Hall*, an 88A Cardiff (Canton) engine, climbs past the ranks of multi-aspect colour light signals and enters Cardiff (General) with the 11.50 am Swansea to Manchester express on 7th April 1962. Transferred to 87F Llanelly in June of the same year, *Gatacre Hall* ended its working life from the unsung shed at 87B Duffryn Yard in December 1963. (R. Picton)

169)	Despite the unkempt appearance, somebody at 85B Gloucester (Horton Road) still had some affection for 1400 Class 0-4-2T No 1440 as the smokebox had been daubed with the slogan 'Chalford King', a reference to the Chalford auto-train services for which these engines had been in command of for so many years. Nearing the end of its 'reign', 1440 was in charge of two trailers and a van, at Gloucester, in April 1963. (Ray Harris)

170)	By coincidence there has been many references to engines based at 82B St. Philip's Marsh within the pages of this album, so we will take one last look at the depot, this time on 23rd May 1963. The fires had been drawn for possibly the last time, from a soon to be withdrawn Castle Class 4-6-0 No 4090 Dorchester Castle, from 88L Cardiff East Dock, dumped inside one of the roundhouses at 82B (N. E. Preedy)

171) 'Dukedog' Class 4-4-0 No 9000 at Cheltenham Spa, Lansdown station, with an S.L.S. railtour from Birmingham, travelling over the former M & SWJR route to Swindon on 14th June 1953. This locomotive was loaned by 89C Machynlleth for the occasion. 9000, built at Swindon in 1936 incorporated parts from Nos 3288 and 3422, and once carried the name *Earl of Mount Edgcumbe*, which was transferred to *Castle* Class 4-6-0 No 5043. (A. N. H. Glover)

172) *Modified Hall* Class 4-6-0 No 6999 *Capel Dewi Hall*, in the yard of its home shed at 83C Westbury, on 26th April 1964. *Capel Dewi Hall* achieved brief fame when *Castle* Class 4-6-0 No 4079 *Pendennis Castle* shed most of her firebars a few miles before Westbury, on the Paddington to Taunton leg of the 'Ian Allan' railtour on 9th May 1964. *Capel Dewi Hall* was commandeered and put in an excellent performance to Taunton. (R. Hennefer)

173) Many of the smaller depots on the Western Region were classed as sub-sheds and some were of moderate size but few came any smaller than Dowlais Central, a one road structure, built by the Brecon and Merthyr Railway and opened in 1898. During B.R. days its parent depot was 88D Merthyr. In steam outside the shed on 21st May 1955 was 5700 Class 0-6-0PT No 4616 (88D). The shed closed in May 1960. (N. L. Browne)

174) Without doubt the most sought after *King* Class 4-6-0 by trainspotters, was No 6026 *King John*, unless you lived on the Plymouth to Paddington route. This 83D Laira (Plymouth) engine was photographed at Newton Abbot with an up express in 1955. *King John* left Laira in February 1960, for 81A Old Oak Common, where it then became a common sight on the Paddington - Birmingham - Wolverhampton - Shrewsbury line. (R. S. Carpenter)

175) The signalman at Pontardulais stands erect with his right arm extended, holding aloft the single line tablet for the driver of 5700 Class 0-6-0PT No 5702, from 87F Llanelly to collect, on 27th May 1956. 5702 was in charge of the 8.30 am local passenger from Llandovery to Llanelly. The smartly kept, compact signalbox, tidy platforms and signal gantries help to complete this fine picture. (N. L. Browne)

176) We take our leave of 'BR Steaming on the Western region' – Volume 3, with this side-view of *Hall* Class 4-6-0 No 4902 *Aldenham Hall*, from 81F Oxford, which had paused at Southall station with an up local passenger train on 4th April 1959. Later transfers took 4902 to 84E Tyseley, 81E Didcot and 83B Taunton, where it was withdrawn from the latter depot in September 1963. Cutting up was provided by Cohens, Morriston, Swansea in May 1964. (F. Hornby)